What is a River?

Monica Hughes

www.raintreepublishers.co.uk
Visit our website to find out more information about **Raintree** books.

To order:
☎ Phone 44 (0) 1865 888112
▤ Send a fax to 44 (0) 1865 314091
▥ Visit the Raintree Bookshop at **www.raintreepublishers.co.uk** to browse our catalogue and order online.

First published in Great Britain by Raintree, Halley Court, Jordan Hill, Oxford OX2 8EJ, part of Harcourt Education.
Raintree is a registered trademark of Harcourt Education Ltd.

Editorial: Catherine Clarke and Sarah Chappelow
Design: Michelle Lisseter
Picture Research: Maria Joannou, Erica Newbery and Kay Altwegg
Production: Amanda Meaden

Originated by Dot Gradations Ltd
Printed and bound in China by South China Printing Company

ISBN 1 844 43647 0 (hardback)
09 08 07 06 05
10 9 8 7 6 5 4 3 2 1

ISBN 1 844 43653 5 (paperback)
10 09 08 07 06
10 9 8 7 6 5 4 3 2 1

British Library Cataloguing in Publication Data
Hughes, Monica
What is a River?. – (The World Around Us)
577.6'4
A full catalogue record for this book is available from the British Library.

Acknowledgements
The publishers would like to thank the following for permission to reproduce photographs: Alamy (Comstock Images) p. **17**; Corbis pp. **6** (Jose Fuste Raga), **9**, **12** (Lynda Richardson), **13**, **15**, **16** (Pat O'Hara), **19** (Natalie Fobes), **20** (Joseph Sohm/Chromosohm Inc.), **22** (Natalie Fobes), **23d** (Lynda Richardson) **23f** (Pat O'Hara); Digital Vision p. **22**; Getty Images (Photodisc) pp. **5**, **7**, **8**, **10**, **11**, **14**, **21**, **22**, **23b**, **23c**, **23e**; Harcourt Education Ltd (Corbis) p. **22**; NHPA (Alan Williams) p. **18**; Robert Harding Picture Library pp. **4**, **23a**.

Cover photograph reproduced with permission of Getty Images (Photodisc).

Every effort has been made to contact copyright holders of any material reproduced in this book. Any omissions will be rectified in subsequent printings if notice is given to the publishers.

The paper used to print this book comes from sustainable resources.

Contents

Some words are shown in bold, **like this.**
You can find them in the glossary on page 23.

Have you seen a river?

Maybe you have seen a small river called a stream.

You might have crossed a bridge from one **bank** to the other.

A river is a **channel** of water that flows to the sea.

There are rivers all over the world.

Where can rivers be found?

Some rivers wind their way through the countryside.

Other rivers flow past the towns and cities built up beside them.

Some rivers flow through mountains or thick forests.

All rivers start from high ground and flow down towards the sea.

What does a river look like?

Sometimes a river is fast-flowing and bubbly.

When it crashes down a waterfall a river can look white and foamy.

Some rivers flow very slowly.

Then, the river may look cloudy and muddy.

How wide is a river?

A river is narrow at its **source**.

Some are so narrow that it is not far from one **bank** across to the other.

Some rivers are wide.

A river gets wider closer to the sea, when more water flows into it.

How deep is a river?

Some rivers are so shallow that you can touch the **river bed**.

A river becomes shallow in hot weather, or when there is no rain.

Some rivers are very deep.

They are so deep that big ships can sail on them.

How long is a river?

Rivers can be different lengths.

Most rivers start as a tiny stream and then join other streams to form longer rivers.

Some rivers are very long.

A river is measured from its **source** to its **mouth**, where it meets the sea.

How do rivers change the land?

As a river flows over the land it moves stones and soil.

Over thousands of years it carves out **banks** and a **valley**.

Sometimes a river breaks its banks and floods the land.

Some floods bring water for farmland, others do lots of damage.

What lives in a river?

Many animals live in the river or on the river **bank**.

Otters make their homes in the river bank, and so do beavers.

The river is home to many kinds of fish.

Different plants also grow in rivers.

How do people use rivers?

We all need water to live, and some of this comes from rivers.

Rivers can be used for travelling by boat.

All over the world there are people who live on or beside a river.

Rivers can also be used for having fun!

Quiz

Which of these animals live in a river or on the river **bank?**

Glossary

bank
side of a river

channel
bottom and sides of a river. The water in a river flows along the channel.

mouth
place where a river flows into the sea

river bed
bottom of a river

source
place where a river begins

valley
low land between hills. Rivers often flow through valleys.

Index

Answer to quiz on page 22

Fish live in rivers. Otters live on the river bank.